LAY PRESIDENCY
AT THE
EUCHARIST?

AFFIRMING CATHOLICISM

H. Benedict Green CR

LAY PRESIDENCY AT THE EUCHARIST?

DARTON·LONGMAN+TODD

Published by Darton, Longman and Todd, 1 Spencer Court, 140–142 Wandsworth High Street, London SW18 4JJ in association with Affirming Catholicism, St Mary-le-Bow, Cheapside, London EC2V 6AU.

ISBN 0–232–52096–8

The views expressed in this booklet are those of the author and do not necessarily reflect any policy of Affirming Catholicism.

Booklets designed by Bet Ayer, phototypeset by Intype, London and printed by Halstan and Co Ltd, Amersham, Bucks.

Affirming Catholicism

Affirming Catholicism has never been and is not intended to be, yet another 'party' within the Church of England or the Anglican Communion but rather a movement of encouragement and hope.

A group of lay people and clergy met together in 1990 to identify that authentic Catholic tradition within the Church which appeared to be under threat. Wider support was expressed at a public meeting on 9 June 1990 in London and at a residential conference in York in July 1991.

Since then Affirming Catholicism has been afforded charitable status. The following statement is extracted from the Trust Deed:

> It is the conviction of many that a respect for scholarship and free enquiry has been characteristic of the Church of England and of the Churches of the wider Anglican Communion from earliest times and is fully consistent with the status of those Churches as part of the Holy Catholic Church. It is desired to establish a charitable educational foundation which will be true both to those characteristics and to the Catholic tradition within Anglicanism ... The object of the foundation shall be the advancement of education in the doctrines and the historical development of the Church of England and the Churches of the wider Anglican Communion, as held by those professing to stand within the Catholic tradition.

In furtherance of these aims and objectives, Affirming Catholicism is producing this series of booklets. The series will encompass two sets of books: one set will attempt to present a clear, well-argued Catholic viewpoint on issues of debate facing the Church at any given time; the other set will cover traditional doctrinal themes. The editor of the series is Jeffrey John; the first four titles in the series were: *Imagining Jesus – An Introduction to the Incarnation* by Lewis Ayres; *Why Women Priests? – The Ordination of Women and the Apostolic Ministry* by Jonathan Sedgwick; *History, Tradition and Change – Church History and the Development of Doctrine* by Peter Hinchliff; *'Permanent, Faithful, Stable' – Christian Same-sex Partnerships* by Jeffrey John. Other titles are: *Politics and the Faith Today – Catholic Social Vision for the 1990s* by Kenneth Leech; *Christ in Ten Thousand Places– A Catholic Perspective on Christian Encounter with Other Faiths* by Michael Ipgrave; *Is the Anglican Church Catholic? – The Catholicity of Anglicanism* by Vincent Strudwick; *Making Present – The Practice of Catholic Life and Liturgy* by Christopher Irvine.

To order these publications individually or on subscription, or for enquiries regarding the aims and activities of Affirming Catholicism write to:

The Secretary
Mainstream
St Mary-le-Bow
Cheapside
London EC2V 6AU

Tel: 071–329 4070

LAY PRESIDENCY
AT THE
EUCHARIST?

There is nothing like a sacramental issue for threatening the stability of the coalition that is the Church of England. In bringing their proposals for 'extended communion' to the General Synod in November 1993[1] the Bishops might have done better to recall how recently and how partially the official Church has accommodated itself to any form of reservation of the Sacrament. With, I think, only a single exception, none of them will have had any personal recollection of the Revised Prayer Book debacle of 1928, when it was the very modest provisions for reservation, more than anything else, that stuck in the throats of the lay opponents of the Book in the Commons and caused it to be thrown out for the second time. Since then, and particularly since the war, there has been something like a tacit agreement to live and let live (of which some Catholics cannot be altogether acquitted of taking unfair advantage in their devotional practice). It is when their acquiescence seems to be taken for granted in proposals that will, as a matter of policy, affect the whole Church that others, Evangelicals in particular, respond with counter-proposals equally unacceptable, as they know, to the opposite camp.

That was the background and the context of the calls for lay presidency that were heard with increasing frequency in the latter part of the Synod debate. Although the problem under discussion was, and remains, a real one, there was unnecessary provocation in the method proposed for dealing with it. If we look into earlier Christian history in this area, the nearest that we get to 'extended communion' is what is called the Liturgy of the Presanctified. This is really a survival from the very early practice of the faithful taking away fragments of the consecrated bread from the Sunday eucharist to communicate themselves at home during the week. When Christians were finally free to build and worship in public churches, this came to be replaced by communion of the congregation from the reserved elements on all days when a full eucharist was not celebrated. That the practice was soon found unsatisfactory is indicated by the fact that it became very rare, surviving in the Christian East only on the Wednesdays and Fridays of Lent, and in the West on Good Friday alone. (This is one of the stock examples of what has been called 'Baumstark's law'[2]: 'the survival of what is ancient in seasons of high liturgical importance.') Roman Catholic practice in our own time in under-priested areas such as rural France or Latin America, to which a good deal of reference was made in the course of the debate, may be perceived as reviving that pattern. In this case the elements which the people will receive have been reserved from the last eucharist celebrated in the church where they are to be administered. The Bishops' report was unwilling to provide for this apart from 'unforeseen emergencies'. The nature of the distinction between extension in place and extension in time, between eucharistic elements consecrated on a previous day in the same place and those consecrated on the same day in a different place, was never made entirely clear. One would have supposed those to whom reservation was acceptable to be happy with both, and those to whom it was repugnant to be happy with neither. A number of contributions to the debate confirmed that the latter at least was indeed the case.

I call the provocation unnecessary because the real objection to the proposals cut across party lines. While the debate was coloured by deep and probably irreconcilable differences on the subject of the reservation of the Sacrament, it would be wrong to see this as the fundamental issue. What was central to the most theologically informed of the contributions[3] was their insistence that to receive communion from elements previously consecrated elsewhere is not to celebrate the eucharist (and there is a real danger that parishioners exposed to the practice over the months of, say, a long interregnum might come to see it as just that). The eucharist is an action – more strictly, a sequence of actions of which the communion is the climax. To divorce it from what has led up to it is to risk obscuring that it is about the death and resurrection of Christ and that our communion with him (and, in him, with one another) rests on our reconciliation to God through him. Dr Christina Baxter spoke for many who would not share her understanding of the eucharistic action and its accompanying symbolism in her impassioned appeal that this fundamental truth should not be obscured.

Dr Paul Avis, who in advance of the debate had offered an admirable summary of the part played by the priest in the eucharistic action in an article contributed to the *Church Times*,[4] confined himself in his speech to another aspect, the nature of the eucharistic community; but he returned in his conclusion to 'the importance of eucharistic presidency'. It is this issue, which was in danger of becoming submerged in the later stages of the debate, that I now want to take up.

As a way in to the theology of it, let us consider an imaginary situation which few, if any, readers will have experienced at first hand, though those whose imagination has been shaped by what they have learned of the Second World War, to say nothing of events since, will have little difficulty in picturing it. There are four Christians together in an internment camp; we will assume that they come from church communities that are in communion with one another. They are aware of their need for the eucharist: they want to celebrate it together, but none of them is a priest. What should they do about it? There are three sorts of answer to that question.

First, there is the hard-line 'Catholic' response: no priest, no eucharist. The absence of a priest is the determining factor. Only the ordained priest has the power to do with the elements of bread and wine that which makes them the sacramental gifts offered and received in the eucharist. We have met this understanding elsewhere; it clearly underlies some of the Vatican's criticisms of the *Final Report* of ARCIC I.[5] It is also substantially the statement of the Tractarian position attributed to Liddon: 'Without a bishop there is no priest; without a priest there is no eucharist; and without the eucharist there is no Church.' This has been widely taught by his successors in the Catholic movement. On this view the only course open to our prisoners is an act of 'spiritual communion', and this is essentially an individual devotional exercise, conveying nothing visibly to the *koinonia*, the shared life in Christ of the little group of Christians struggling to live out their discipleship in circumstances of great difficulty. Since an essential part of what constitutes and defines sacraments is that they are 'outward and visible signs', the suggested devotion is clearly no substitute.

Secondly, and at the opposite end of the spectrum, there is what I may call the popular Protestant understanding of the question: any Christian, by virtue of his baptismal share in the priesthood of all believers, may preside over the eucharistic worship of his community. On this view each of the four prisoners will take his turn to preside and none will be greater or less than another in this matter.

The third alternative is that the four should choose one of their number to lead and represent them in the sacramental action, to be the visible focus of their unity in Christ, and this will involve rather more than addressing God on their behalf. The other side of the coin is that he also speaks to them on God's behalf; or, as the Lima statement[6] put it, he is to 'call the community to submit to the authority of Jesus Christ'. This means that he cannot have the ministry of the eucharist without the ministry to the Church, of which the little band is, in however irregular or 'extraordinary' a sense, a local embodiment; and this should mean that their 'election' of him is followed by prayer that God will confirm their choice by bestowing the gifts requisite for the exercise of such a ministry. This will be effectively ordination for and within the limits of the situation that called for it. As to the lack of a person competent to lead the essential prayer on behalf of the whole Church (i.e. a bishop), the plea of necessity, real necessity, is a strong one in sacramental matters. In the event of a return to normality its effects would either lapse with that situation, or require some form of integration into the regular ministry of the Church. But that aspect really lies outside the scope of the parable as I have constructed it, though it will not be wholly irrelevant to my eventual conclusion.

Let us look a little more closely at these three approaches, and try to uncover the theological presuppositions that underlie them.

(i)   The first represents an understanding of priesthood that did not really emerge completely until the early Middle Ages. This view saw priesthood in terms not (as formerly) of a ministerial relationship to the Church as the Body of Christ, but of an unmediated relationship to the eucharistic Body of Christ, which his ordination conferred on him the power to 'confect' and offer. As Henri de Lubac showed in *Corpus Mysticum*,[7] a fascinating and remarkable book which still remains untranslated and little known outside the ranks of specialists, the expressions *corpus verum* (true/real body) and *corpus mysticum* (mystical body) swapped meanings at the beginning of this period. When the early Fathers spoke of the 'Body of Christ' without qualification they had meant the Church; by his 'mystical Body' they meant his 'Body in the mysteries', that is, his sacramental Body received in the eucharist. But in medieval usage the 'real' Body is the historical flesh of Jesus Christ, miraculously made present and accessible in the eucharist, and the Church becomes the 'mystical' Body, the term 'mystical' being understood in much the same sense as in the expression 'the mystical sense of Scripture', i.e. non-literal, not readily accessible, even a hint of 'not quite real'. It now belongs more in the realm of contemporary legal fictions like 'the King's Two Bodies' than in a living theology of the people of God. As is well enough known, medieval Catholicism worked out a developed theology of the sacraments, but no comparably developed theology of the Church (a subject that tended to get left to canon lawyers). The eucharist is thus no longer something that the Church does with and through the priest, but something the priest does on his own, with the people passive spectators if present, and often with barely even a token presence of the Church with him. The effects of this development are still with us when we speak, even in jest, of the priest 'saying the magic words', and in many other ways.

(ii) The 'priesthood of all believers', a Reformation formulation of the teaching of 1 Peter 2:9 and Revelation 5:10, was a protest against the idea of a class of Christians with special powers and means of access to God denied to the rest; but its emphasis was upon the 'equality of individuals, not on the corporate character' of that priesthood.[8] In this, as in the usual pattern of their worship, where Protestantism tended in practice to substitute a clericalism of the pulpit for the medieval clericalism of the altar, the Reformers, as Gregory Dix was constantly reminding us, were more medieval in their initial assumptions than their successors have always cared to admit. The reference of the two texts cited above is clearly a corporate one, to the whole company of the redeemed (and in the case of Revelation 5:10 clearly in the context of worship). But the form of the expression used by the Reformers has in fact tended, both in their own time and since, to what has been called 'a ruinous individualism'; it has too readily been construed as 'the priesthood of every (or indeed of any) believer'. As applied to the presiding role in worship, it simply becomes the medieval understanding of priesthood with a minus sign in front of it. It asks what a priest is supposed to have power to do, and then goes on to say that any Christian 'can do' it. A particular form of this confusion, often heard at present, is that which asks: if a lay person can baptise, why can he or she not celebrate the other gospel sacrament also? It is a question that deserves a proper answer, and we will digress in order to offer one, but it has to be said first that in this form it is a question *mal posée*, for it asks what a lay person in him- or herself can do, by comparison with what a priest in himself can do, and this is to start from the medieval account of the latter. We should rather ask: how is the Church's understanding of a sacrament expressed in its practice, and what is the part played in this by the individual minister or lay person?

What then of lay baptism? It has to be said first that tradition has not been universally in favour of it even in an emergency. Classical Reformation thinking was generally against it, and that not solely from political considerations such as those connected with the practice of the 'popish baptism of midwives' in Elizabethan England. The real objection was to do with baptism as a public rite of the Church, to be celebrated in the presence of the worshipping community, not just the child and its sponsors. In this respect the Reformers' claim to be restoring the practice of the primitive Church was largely justified. But before the medieval distortions there was already a divergence between the practice of East and West. The Orthodox East has never subscribed to the position that any Christian can perform the rite of baptism. Partly this is the consequence of their never having split up the sequence of the developed rites of initiation (certain of which have always been held to require the ministry of a priest, if not a bishop). Partly it is because Orthodoxy has developed a strongly hieratic view of the role of the priest within the one liturgy of the Church (very different from the hieratic individualism of the priest in the medieval West). It may be mentioned in passing that in the Orthodox rite of marriage the minister of this sacrament is the priest who blesses the couple, not, as in the later Western tradition, the bridegroom and bride themselves.

The divergence over baptism probably goes back beyond any of this. In Syria from a very early date baptism was administered with a Trinitarian formula, 'X is baptised in the name of the Father and of the Son and of the Holy Spirit'. Whether this was derived from Matthew 28:19 or, as I have argued elsewhere,[9] a very early interpolation into the gospel text (before its reception into the canon of the New Testament) from contemporary liturgical practice in the region in which it first saw the light, it must represent Syrian practice in the years leading up to AD 100. The expectation would have been that such a solemn pronouncement would fall to the official local leader of the church – or, as he soon became, the bishop. In what became the Latin West the picture is different: in Rome at least, a formula pronounced by the baptiser at the moment of baptism is unknown before the seventh century. The one who spoke was the candidate himself, and his words were his response to the threefold interrogatory form of the Trinitarian baptismal creed (in essentials what we now know as the Apostles' Creed). At some point (I would guess mid-second century, but the date is of no great import) this credal affirmation had superseded an earlier Christological formula such a 'Jesus is Lord' (see Romans 10:9, 1 Corinthians 12:3). In this version of the early practice the baptiser is simply the witness to the candidate's profession of faith; the latter and the water are the essentials of the sacrament. The East bears witness to this in its own way by its use of the passive formula 'X is baptised . . .'; and we may also recall St Paul's disclaimer in 1 Corinthians 1 of any special relationship between himself and the few to whom he had been obliged to administer the sacrament personally.

We can now go on to ask: what feature of the eucharistic liturgy played the corresponding part to that of the creed in baptism? It is important to ask the question that way round. If one inverts it and asks what feature in the developed baptismal liturgy corresponds to the eucharistic anaphora one is likely to get the answer 'the blessing of the water', which did indeed develop as a kind of counterpart in form to the anaphora, but has not been seen as essential to baptism in the way that the latter is to the eucharist. The answer is evidently not the Nicene Creed, a latecomer to the rite which, not always for reputable reasons,[10] got itself inserted at various relatively insignificant points in the liturgies of different churches in East and West. The feature which corresponds to the part of the creed in baptism is actually the eucharistic prayer itself, which expressed in doxological form (i.e. addressed to God and giving him the glory) the faith of the worshipping Church, just as the faith of the individual convert was expressed in the creed to which he or she responded.

The representative character of the function of pronouncing this is not something inherent in individual baptismal status as such. It is the whole Church that is priestly, as it is the whole Church that is indwelt by the Spirit. Where one individual has, in the nature of things, to speak for all, there is a focusing upon him, by the operation of the Spirit, of that which is true of the whole. Representative in this connection does not mean vicarious: what he says he says on behalf of all, and they in heart and mind say it with him, and assent with their Amen. As Schillebeeckx has put it in the conclusion to his account of how the Church's ministry reached its original settled form: 'Specialization by individuals of what belongs communally to everyone is from a sociological perspective and, in the case of a church group, from an ecclesial perspective, an obvious development in any group formation. If there is no specialized concentration of what is important to everyone, in the long run the community suffers as a result.'[11] Thus the Great Thanksgiving (and it alone; all handling of the elements can in principle be delegated or shared) has been reserved to the ordained president (bishop or presbyter) as representative of the priesthood of the whole Body.

(iii) We can now return to our opening parable. The third of the responses to the situation envisaged there corresponds with the authentic tradition of the Church, from the time when a settled pattern of ministry first emerges into the light of day (sometime in the second century, although some churches came to it earlier than others). Before the labours of missionary bishops led to the creation of territorially extended dioceses – and local presbyters came to lack education and to be subject to the control of local thanes and lordlings – presidency at the eucharist clearly belonged with two other things: the ministry of the word (involving a homily at each celebration) and pastoral responsibility for the worshipping community. The Council of Chalcedon in AD 451 (better known for its statement concerning the nature of the Incarnation) also reaffirmed as the Church's authentic practice that none should be ordained presbyter except in relation to a particular, territorially defined, Christian community (hence ordination to a 'title', still standard practice in the Church of England).[12] How the eucharist became, in part, detached from the other two is a complicated story which cannot be told in full here. But it can hardly be regarded as other than a deformation; and this in itself is a warning against any shortsighted separation of them now.

To those who hold that the pattern of ministry which emerged in the course of the second century was, however obscure the process of the transition, 'in the providence of God',[13] the part played by this ministry in the celebration of the eucharist belongs to the settled sacramental practice of the Church. But both on account of the Reformation principle *sola scriptura* and because the reception of charismatic gifts, never totally dormant for very long in the history of the Church, has enjoyed a revival in the mainline churches in our own time, there will be voices raised to insist that the formal ministry that emerged was itself a restriction of the freedom of the Spirit that characterised the Church of the apostolic age, and that we should now look behind it to what is found in the New Testament. I want to keep open the lines of communication and dialogue with such voices; the reservations that I have are due to the sheer limitations of our knowledge of what actually went on.

We have in fact no narrative account of the celebration of a eucharist anywhere in the New Testament. The few possible allusions in the Acts of the Apostles[14] are so vague and devoid of detail that it is impossible to be sure that it is the Lord's Supper that they are actually speaking about, let alone to establish in detail what happened at it. We owe the Pauline account in 1 Corinthians 11:23ff. to the fact that some of the more affluent Christians in Corinth had been misbehaving at it! Even so, all that Paul gives is an excerpt from his original instruction about it (very precious, since the substance of it, as he insists, is what he received from those who were Christians before him: that is to say, the tradition), and some guidance and warning about right reception. More generally, the only first-hand evidence for the day-to-day life and operation of the earliest Church is the authentic letters of Paul, and these were not entirely typical in their own time, even though the stream that they represent became in time the mainstream. (Professor Henry Chadwick observed in the first of his inaugural lectures[15] that 'if there is any man who more than any other man may be regarded by the historian as the founder of the papacy, that man is surely St Paul'). Moreover, the greater and most detailed part of the evidence comes from the Corinthian correspondence, and Corinth seems to have been, even by the standards of its own time, an unusually excitable church, so we cannot safely take it as entirely typical. It follows from this that what these writings offer is a series of windows, of varying sizes, on the daily life of the earliest Church. Precious as they are, you cannot make a panorama by piecing them together; still less do they provide bricks or blocks to build a model for replication in our own time.

I am speaking of the period in which there were no local ordained ministers. The talk in the undisputed Pauline letters is (with the exception of apostles, who came in from outside, and prophets, some at least of whom did the same) of ministries rather than of ministers, and of those as charisms, free gifts bestowed by the Spirit at his own good pleasure (see 1 Corinthians 12:4–11, 28). Corinthian Christians are urged to 'seek earnestly the best gifts, especially that you may prophesy' (14:1), but clearly not to claim them before they have been given. It was certainly not a case of what one can do, all may. A charismatic free-for-all is hardly the name of the game here.

Who, then, would have presided over the celebration of the Lord's Supper in the house churches of Corinth when the apostle was not around? The short answer is that we don't know. Since we have no narrative account of what happened at it, hard evidence is just not available. But if we go on to ask more speculatively which gifts of the Spirit might have been thought to qualify a local Christian for this role, the indirect evidence points us in two directions.

The first of these is the householder. Whether or not the Last Supper was an actual passover meal (the world of scholarship continues to debate this point[16]), the eucharist is rooted in the traditional practice at Jewish domestic meals and its central prayer in the thanksgivings which were recited at them. The duty of pronouncing these ordinarily fell on the father of the family, and the natural president of a house church[17] would have been the owner of the house in which, by his invitation, it met. 1 Corinthians 14:23 indicates that in Paul's time there were occasions on which the whole church in Corinth assembled in one place for worship. The wording of 11:20 implies that the Lord's Supper was one of these, and Romans 16:23 (written from Corinth) speaks of Gaius as 'host to the whole church' (his may well have been the only house large enough to accommodate them all). As the church there continued to expand it is likely that no available house would have served that purpose. The letter of Clement of Rome[18] to the church of Corinth at the end of the century (both of them churches which had not yet developed the system of government by a single bishop) defined the function of the (plural) *episkopoi* as 'offering the gifts'.[19] In the light of what has already been said, this suggests that they were still the eucharistic presidents of the house churches, rather than that they took turns at presiding at a single local eucharist. The name of their office on the other hand (already found in the opening greeting at Philippians 1:1) which means 'overseers', connotes pastoral responsibility and implies that the liturgy of 'offering the gifts' belonged with this.[20]

The other indication lies in the character of the eucharistic prayer itself. We know that whereas the form of a Jewish *eucharistia* followed a generally recognised pattern, its content was improvised. This seems to have continued through the second century, if not later (witness the famous account of eucharistic worship written at Rome about AD 150 by the Christian apologist Justin Martyr,[21] in which the 'president' is said to give thanks 'to the best of his ability'). The early improvised character of the prayer has left its mark on the Roman liturgy and its derivatives in the persistence of the variable preface. This used to be called, in some English editions of the old (Pian) Roman Missal, 'the Preface to the Canon'. That is a fascinating illustration of bad etymological currency driving out good. The true meaning of the word *praefatio* is not something prefixed but something spoken out loud; it came eventually to denote the initial section of the prayer which continued to be audible after the rest (everything following the *Sanctus*) had become silent. But before that regrettable development it meant the whole prayer, and there are good reasons for supposing that it renders the Greek *propheteia*, 'prophecy', and thus that the latter was a word used to designate the eucharistic prayer when the language of the Roman liturgy was still Greek (as it remained, in part at least, until the fourth century).

Now if Paul exhorts the Christians of Corinth to 'desire earnestly the best gifts, and especially that you may prophesy' (1 Corinthians 14:1) he also gives prophets the place of honour next to apostles in his list of those whose position in the Church is constituted by the gifts they have received through the Spirit (12:28); and this persists in the later, probably post-Pauline list in Ephesians 4:11, where the emphasis seems to be on minist*ers* rather than minist*ries*. In the *Didache* (or *Teaching of the Twelve Apostles*), a pseudonymous document which it is impossible to date with certainty, but likely to belong in its final form to the second century, visiting itinerant prophets are not only invited to recite the prayer over the gifts but encouraged to extend it for longer than is customary.[22] And it has been suggested that the prominence in the Church of charismatic prophetic personalities like Ignatius and Polycarp contributed on its liturgical side to the gathering up of episcopal functions into a single monarchical bishop, who was regarded as a successor to the prophets as well as to the apostles.[23]

In this connection it is worth spending a little time on the ancient exchange in the liturgy, *'Dominus vobiscum'/'Et cum spiritu tuo'*. I give it in the Latin to show that there (as in the underlying Greek) the verb 'to be' is suppressed, so that there is no clear indication of what 'mood' of it is intended. For centuries, in the West at least, it has been taken as subjunctive, expressing a wish. On that interpretation it is no more than a benevolent greeting, stronger than 'Good morning', perhaps, but by the same token slightly weaker than 'Goodbye' (i.e. 'God be wi' ye'; compare the French 'adieu'). But in our earliest liturgical texts it is not used as an opening greeting to the congregation; it is an introduction to prayer in which the president is going to lead the people (as in the eucharistic prayer) or to sum up with a collect (as in the intercessions). It thus conveys a transaction without which the prayer cannot take place, a mutual recognition. But of what? Certainly of something that is the case (so the verb must be indicative: 'The Lord *is* with you'). But what is meant by this? That was the question that a theologian of the Dutch Reformed Church,[24] now departed this life, put to himself when the liturgical reformers of his Church were proposing to introduce this little dialogue into its worship. He went into the biblical background and found that the idea that it conveyed was something very potent indeed. In the Old Testament, to say that the Lord 'was with' somebody, e.g. Joseph, Moses, Joshua, Gideon, Samuel, Saul, David, Jeremiah, meant that he was beside them in power as a protecting, supporting and encouraging presence. This again is the meaning in the Great Commission at the end of St Matthew's Gospel, itself closely based on Old Testament models, where the Risen Christ promises to 'be with' his disciples until the end of time. But (our theologian went on to argue) in post-resurrection settings in the New Testament it conveys the dynamic presence of 'the Lord the Spirit' (as in 2 Corinthians 3:17–18).[25] For a prospective eucharistic president to say 'The Lord is with you' to his congregation would signify that he recognises the presence of the Spirit of Christ among them – that they are, so to say, the 'real thing', a true church and not a counterfeit. Compare 1 Corinthians 14:25, where Paul pictures the response of an imaginary visiting outsider to a well-conducted prayer meeting at which prophecy is encouraged: 'falling on his face he will worship God and declare that God is really among you'.

What then is conveyed by the people's reply? Here I am afraid that the compilers of the Alternative Service Book have done us a disservice. Their version of the 'indicative' interpretation of *Dominus vobiscum*, 'The Lord is here' was a gesture in the right direction, but the response, 'His Spirit is with us', does no more than repeat it, with a hint of self-congratulation. The whole idea of an exchange between president and people is lost. The president has declared to the people his recognition that by his Spirit the Lord is present and at work among them; the people have now to respond to this. The response 'And with your spirit' conveys their recognition of the authentic charism[26] that he brings to the celebration of God's redemptive work in the great thanksgiving – they acknowledge that he will speak by the Spirit as he speaks for them. Their recognition is not of course the source of his gift, for the enabling grace of ministry, any ministry, does not come from below. But if they are truly a community indwelt and led by the Spirit, they will have the 'mind of Christ', and accordingly the capacity to discern the gifts that he through the Spirit bestows on individuals. There is a clear continuity between this and the later settled practice of the Church, in which its ministers were chosen from below (elected by the faithful) but ordained from above (i.e. with prayer to God for the bestowal of the requisite gifts and charisms).

It is interesting that the earliest attestation of this dialogue formula is found in a specimen eucharistic prayer for use by a newly ordained bishop presiding in that capacity for the first time.[27] By then, though (early third century) it could well have become a regular feature of the liturgy; formulas like that commonly become fixed while the prayers still remain variable.

But it would have been particularly appropriate in the case of a visiting celebrant. We can readily imagine it being used by the great prophet-bishop and future martyr Polycarp on the occasion when he visited Rome and was invited to preside at the eucharist of that church,[28] or by the visiting prophets that we meet in the *Didache*. If I hesitate to claim it for the Church of the New Testament itself, that is only for want of explicit evidence. Comparable formulas can be found there;[29] but, more importantly, the theology underlying it clearly belongs to the time of creative origins, when the young Church was simultaneously experiencing a new quality of life in the Spirit and seeking to make sense of it in terms inherited from the scriptures of the old Israel.

I have drawn out the implications of this venerable little survival from primitive liturgy at some length, because it has lessons for us that ought not to be lost. First, that responsibility for leading a church's eucharistic worship was from the beginning a very serious matter, far too serious to be shared out between all and sundry even among the baptised. Secondly, that if I am right in inferring that the natural persons to assume this ministry in apostolic times (in the absence, often prolonged, of apostles) were the leaders of house churches and those with recognised prophetic gifts, it will be natural also to see the former as the regular and the latter as the occasional practitioners of it. The normal president is the pastor of the flock, and the person to whom he gives way on occasion is the one more qualified than himself – the inspired minister of the word. That is what the charism of the early Christian prophet amounted to, and it was a two-way affair. Finding words to convey the word spoken by the Spirit to the Church and finding words to express the Church's response in praise and thanksgiving were the obverse and the reverse sides of the same charismatic gift.

As I have said already, the New Testament does not offer us models that we can simply reproduce, but insights that can be applied to our later situation. The ministry of the word does not now normally consist, in the experience of most of us, of inspired messages from on high. I am not excluding the prophetic, but it is now to be recognised for what it is by contrast with what is generally heard, by its occasional character. (I fear that the Pentecostal insistence on it as the norm only trivialises, too often, the content of the allegedly prophetic message.) The fundamental reason for this has been the formation of the Christian canon of Scripture, the addition of the New Testament to the Old. This was a necessary control as the widening Church drew apart from its Jewish matrix and the white-hot experience of the first generation was succeeded by a level of insight that, however genuine, was necessarily second hand.

The content of the eucharistic thanksgiving underwent a similar metamorphosis. While the original habit of variation was not immediately changed, inspired extemporisation gave way to studied composition and ultimately to a fixed and authorised text. It is significant that in the days when that first began to come about it was often great episcopal teachers of the Church, true successors in their own way to the 'prophetic' bishops of the second century – among whom St Basil is surely preeminent – who set their minds to the composition of anaphoras, and that they concentrated their attention not on the nuances of offering and acceptance and consecration with which our own revisers have had to be preoccupied, but on the whole sweep of the economy of salvation for which God was to be praised.[30] What had begun as a charismatic act of Christ in the Spirit (the great thanksgiving) was thus transformed into a representative act of Christ in the Body; and the emergence over the same period of the settled form of the Church's ministry, in which eucharistic presidency was linked both with pastoral responsibility and ministry of the word, was hardly coincidental.

It is idle to suppose that this particular clock can be put back, or that if the attempt was made to do so, charismatic fervour would be automatically matched with charismatic wisdom and insight. The great scholar Armitage Robinson warned many years ago against 'trying to live in the apostolic age without the unifying control of the apostles.'[31] It is possible to argue historically (though I have yet to meet with convincing grounds) that the eucharist was of less importance to the Church of the New Testament than it had become at least by the following century and has remained for the larger part of mainstream Christianity ever since. It is not possible to maintain that importance (which the clamour for lay presidency presupposes) and at the same time to treat the standing of the person leading it as a matter of no consequence. The way forward is not to break out of the given structures, but to ask what sort of modification of them is possible from within.

The first thing to be observed is that the two-tier episcopal structure of ministry which we have inherited from that original consolidation leaves room for a flexibility which is not easily achieved in a one-tier system. In the office of a bishop the ministries of the word and of the sacraments and of the pastoral care of the faithful are brought together: the teaching and proclamation of saving truth, the provision of sacramental grace, and the inspiration, support and discipline of the membership of the Church belong finally with him. 'The buck stops here.' While he shares these responsibilities with the presbyters of his diocese, he will not necessarily do so in equal proportions with all of them. We need therefore to consider to what extent they may be separable. Compare these three models: (a) the medieval chantry priest; (b) the ordained academic theologian who is not simultaneously a college or university chaplain; (c) the village *pappas* of the Orthodox tradition in Greece.

Priest (a), so far as his 'liturgy' (and his visible means of support) goes, has neither preaching nor pastoral responsibility. This is plainly unacceptable, and it is to this situation that the pejorative expression 'mass priest' really applies. Priest (b) is a kind of non-stipendiary minister; as a theologian he will find himself called upon for preaching and as an available priest for leading the eucharist, but the two roles may not have any integral connection for him, nor will he get pastoral ministry unless he looks for it. Though ordained, he will need his bishop's licence for all three. But if he shows no disposition for pastoral work of any sort, that raises the question why he should need to be ordained at all. Ordination is no necessary qualification for the study and communication of theology (outside the senior positions in the universities of Oxford and Durham), even in the ecclesiastical as opposed to the purely academic field, and lay status, even in the more clericalised ecclesiastical traditions, no bar to it. Priest (c) has traditionally been a person elevated from below: a respected local figure, it may be the village schoolmaster, or a farmer or craftsman (always a married man). His job is to celebrate the liturgy and care for the people; his training for it will usually have been elementary, and he will not preach or hear confessions, provision for these being made at diocesan level – the former being often the responsibility of trained lay theologians. But while he does not preach formally, he will still, if his pastoral ministry is a reality, have both the opportunity and the obligation to speak for God in the course of it, and will do so with an authority which (in the English situation) a Reader who can turn out a polished sermon will not necessarily share.[32]

The implications of these facts are in line with those suggested by our excursion into apostolic and sub-apostolic Christianity. In principle, presidency at the eucharist belongs, as we have seen, both with ministry of the word and with pastoral responsibility. But if unavoidable circumstances compel a choice between them, the bottom line is the pastoral one. This is not to underplay the importance of the word, but rather to say that it does not disappear where there is no regular preacher; the scriptures will still be read, and pastoral letters from 'higher up' expounding them can be read too. As we have seen in the case of the Greek Orthodox *pappas*, an inability to preach formally does not mean that the pastor has no message for his people, but only that he will have to communicate it in other, usually more private, ways. A regular visit from the bishop, or a priest to whom he entrusts this ministry to preside and preach could also, if taken with proper seriousness, do much to offset the shortfall.

Where the argument is leading will by now be becoming clearer. The eucharist is at the heart of the life of any local church that really understands itself as such and provision must be made for regular celebration of it. Yet the office of presiding at it ought not to be regularly divorced from pastoral responsibility at some level for those who will participate in it. The exercise of this should involve at least prior acceptance by the people at the receiving end, if not indeed an initial approach from them. It will also call for a commissioning with prayer and laying on of hands, for which a bishop's licence is not by itself an acceptable substitute. In essence this would be ordination to a form of the presbyterate which, however, need not and should not imply translation to the ranks of the professional clergy. However difficult this may be to get across to the majority of our fellow countrymen, a priest is not necessarily, in that sense, a clergyman. Such a person would be comparable to a presbyter in the Church before the time of the emperor Theodosius, who (rather than Constantine) was responsible for giving the clergy civil rank.[33] It has to be admitted that the idea answers most readily to the needs of socially homogeneous groups like the base communities in Holland, on whose behalf Schillebeeckx (unsuccessfully) argued for it, or their counterparts in the cities of Latin America.[34] It does presuppose a local Christian community with a degree of self-awareness and shared enthusiasm, one that knows where it is going. It is these that ought not to be held back for lack of authorised pastoral leadership and the possibility of celebrating their own eucharist.

Is there anything to correspond to this in our existing provisions? There is, though it is relatively little known outside the deliberations of those with special responsibility for the ministry in a few dioceses and at Church House. This is the Local Non-Stipendiary Ministry (LNSM), originally known as the Local Ordained Ministry (LOM). It aims to identify, call (with the initial impetus coming, to a much greater degree than is presently the case with the full-time ministry, from the local Church) and train locally candidates who will be not only self-supporting, like other NSM's but expected to continue ministering in the local communities from which they have come. After upwards of twenty years of thought, discussion and limited experiment, four separate diocesan schemes are now operative. A useful review and comparison of them by a working party was published by The Advisory Board for Ministry in 1992.[35] I do not know how many candidates from this quarter have now been ordained. Reservations and hesitations about the idea have been expressed on a number of grounds. Some, Archbishop Michael Ramsey among them, have feared the setting up of a class of 'mass priests' and a consequent weakening of the bond between word and sacrament. Others, rightly insisting that ordination is to the ministry of the whole Church and not only to a single congregation, have raised the spectre, to which the history of non-stipendiary ministry in the Church of England so far gives some substance, of men and women with a lower standard of professional training using it as a back door into the ranks of the full-time stipendiary ministry.

Enough has already been said above about the first of these objections. As to the second, it would be truer to Catholic tradition to say that a person is ordained to the ministry of the whole Church as embodied in the local eucharistic community. As the canon of the Council of Chalcedon mentioned earlier makes clear his ordination does not confer on him a prescriptive right to total mobility, but only as far as a bishop shall in future permit, license or institute him. The problems which present-day mobility raises for those ordained to a local ministry on the terms here envisaged are real, but by no means insuperable, given clear guidelines and a firm diocesan discipline. The future ministry of a LNSM who moved would not be ruled out, but it would need to be suspended until he could command the same kind of confidence in his new local community as had brought about his call to ordination in the old one. In any case, as things are now, with too many stipendiary clergy chasing too few jobs, the pressures are going to be in the opposite direction.

So to my conclusion. I cannot see that presiding at the eucharist, which is the characteristic sacramental action of a local worshipping community, is any more separable from the ministry of an ordained priest than is the pastoral care and support of that community as a whole. It is thus not part of the charism of every baptised Christian (whose gifts of ministry in certain situations may well nevertheless surpass the pastor's own). But it is hardly enough to say this and then ignore the pressures that have produced the demand for lay presidency. In so far as the Church of England is a eucharistic church (and to a Catholic, Affirming no less than Latinising, that is of the essence, whatever the shortfall in practice), if it is to remain one yet continue with plans (which may yet turn out to have been shortsighted) to reduce the numbers of the full-time clergy, it must take seriously the need for LNSM, get its understanding of it in better focus, and prepare nationwide and as a matter of urgency to integrate it into its pastoral strategy. Failure to do this could lead to an increase of unilateral action, perhaps not only by those who already sit lightest to their oath of canonical obedience, and release a genie from the bottle that would be difficult, not to say impossible, to put back. And that could finally destroy the unity of the Church of England.

Notes

[1] General Synod, *Report of Proceedings*, 24.3 (November 1993), pp. 891–916.

[2] Anton Baumstark (1872–1948), see his *Comparative Liturgy* (ET by F. L. Cross) London: Mowbray, 1958, p. 27.

[3] I would include in this, in adition to those named below, the speech by Canon Roger Greenacre.

[4] Paul Avis, in the *Church Times*, 10 September 1993.

[5] The text can be found in *One in Christ*, 26 (1992), pp. 38–46. On the present topic see especially pp. 43–45.

[6] *Baptism, Eucharist and Ministry* (Faith and Order Paper No. 3): WCC, Geneva, 1983, p. 21.

[7] H. de Lubac SJ, *Corpus Mysticum*, Paris: Aubier 1949. Cf. E. Schillebeeckx OP, *The Church with a Human Face*, London: SCM, 1985, pp. 193–94.

[8] See G.R. Evans, *Problems of Authority in the Reformation Debates*, Cambridge UP, 1992, pp. 218–19.

[9] I have argued for this position in an essay contributed to Rowan Williams (ed.), *The Making of Orthodoxy* [Essays in honour of Henry Chadwick], Cambridge UP, 1989, pp. 124–41.

[10] The story of how it secured a foothold in the Byzantine rite, as recounted by Dom Gregory Dix, *The Shape of the Liturgy*, London: Dacre, 1945, p. 486, loses nothing in the telling.

[11] Schillebeeckx, op. cit., pp. 121–22.

[12] Canon 6. See Schillebeeckx, op. cit. pp. 154–56.

[13] See the argument of Austin Farrer in his preface to the second edition of K. E. Kirk (ed.), *Apostolic Ministry*, London: Hodder, 1957, p. vi.

[14] See Acts 2:42; 16:34; 20:11; 27:35.

[15] H. Chadwick, *The Circle and the Ellipse* [Inaugural Lecture as Regius Professor of Divinity in the University of Oxford UP], Oxford 1960, p. 1.

[16] The best known protagonist of the passover view of the Last Supper has been Joachim Jeremias, *The Eucharistic Words of Jesus*, London 1963; but neither in his lifetime nor posthumously has his position commanded majority support among specialists.

[17] On the part played by house churches in Corinth see Wayne Meeks, *The First Urban Christians*, Yale UP, 1983, pp. 76–77, 221 n. 7.

[18] Clement has been traditionally represented as bishop of Rome, the third in succession to the apostle Peter. This cannot now be sustained. The letter that bears his name (though not as part of its text) manages to say quite a lot about the ministry without a single allusion to a monarchical bishop, and the letters of Ignatius (traditionally dated c.115, but quite possibly later) name the bishops of the churches in Asia to which they are addressed, but his letter to the Romans is silent about any such personage. A remark in the *Shepherd* of Hermas (Roman, probably middle second century, though some now put it earlier) hints that a person named Clement acted as 'foreign correspondent' of the Roman church (see Hermas, *Vision*, 2.4., and this fits the internal evidence of the letter.

[19] *The Letter of Clement of Rome to the Corinthians*, 44. The earlier patristic texts cited in this tract can be consulted in a collection such as H. Bettenson, *The Early Christian Fathers*, Oxford UP, 1956, or (with the exception of Justin) in any edition of the *Apostolic Fathers*, such as *Early Christian Writers* (Penguin Classics), Harmondsworth, 1968.

[20] The same situation must have obtained in the much larger city and church of Rome. By the time that the system of a single monarchical bishop established itself there (see note 18 above) the number of worship centres in the city would have been too large to handle without retaining the services of the former *episkopoi*, even if under another name. The curious custom of the *fermentum* (the fragment of consecrated bread sent from the altar of the church where the Pope was presiding to each of the other churches in the city, to be dropped in the chalice after the

consecration) looks suspiciously like an attempt to impose a symbolic unity upon a pre-existent plurality.

[21] Justin Martyr, *First Apology*, 67 (Bettenson, p. 86).

[22] *Didache*, 10 (Bettenson, p. 71).

[23] This was the suggestion of Arnold Ehrhardt, *The Apostolic Succession*, London: Lutterworth, 1953, pp. 90–92.

[24] W.C. van Unnik, '*Dominus vobiscum*: the background of a liturgical formula' in A.J.B. Higgins (ed.), *New Testament Essays* [in memory of T.W. Manson], Manchester UP, 1959, pp. 270–305.

[25] ibid., pp. 293–95.

[26] van Unnik, (ibid., p. 292) accepts that 'spirit' here denotes a person's charism, not a part of his natural make-up, citing 2 Tim 4:22. Note that for the probably post-Pauline author of that text Timothy's charism is, it would seem, the product of an act of ordination; cf. 2:6; also 1 Tim 4:14 (where the word *propheteia* evidently means the prayer said over him – a parallel to the eucharistic anaphora).

[27] Hippolytus, *The Apostolic Tradition*, iv.3 (ed. G. Dix and H. Chadwick, London: SPCK, 1968, p. 7).

[28] Eusebius, *History of the Church*, v.24.17 (ed. K. Lake), Loeb Classical Library, London: Heineman, 1926, p. 498.

[29] In addition to 2 Tim 4:22 (note 26 above) see Gal 6:18; Phil 4:23; Philem 25.

[30] In recent years the Liturgical Commission has handsomely redressed the balance; see especially the provision of new proper prefaces in *The Promise of His Glory*, London: Church House Publishing, 1990.

[31] J.A. Robinson, 'The Christian Ministry in the Apostolic and sub-Apostolic period', in H.B. Swete (ed.), *The Early History of the Church and Ministry*, London: Macmillan, 1916, p. 9.

[32] I owe this thought to the essay by W. Jacob, 'The Development of Local Non-

Stipendiary Ministry', in Mark Hodge (ed.), *Non-Stipendiary Ministry of the Church of England*, CIO 1993, p. 105.

[33] Schillebeeckx, op. cit., pp. 141–42.

[34] Schillebeeckx, *Ministry*, London: SCM 1980, pp. 108–10, 136–42.

[35] *A Review of LNSM Schemes*: ABM Ministry Paper No. 4., CIO, November 1992.